THE OFFICIAL CELTIC ANNUAL 2016

Written by Joe Sullivan & Martin Dalziel
Designed by Chris Dalrymple

CONT

ENTS

CLUB HONOURS

SCOTTISH LEAGUE WINNERS [46 TIMES]

1892/93, 1893/94, 1895/96, 1897/98,
1904/05, 1905/06, 1906/07, 1907/08,
1908/09, 1909/10, 1913/14, 1914/15,
1915/16, 1916/17, 1918/19, 1921/22,
1925/26, 1935/36, 1937/38, 1953/54,
1965/66, 1966/67, 1967/68, 1968/69,
1969/70, 1970/71, 1971/72, 1972/73,
1973/74, 1976/77, 1978/79, 1980/81,
1981/82, 1985/86, 1987/88, 1997/98,
2000/01, 2001/02, 2003/04, 2005/06,
2006/07, 2007/08, 2011/12, 2012/13,
2013/14, 2014/15

SCOTTISH CUP WINNERS [36 TIMES]

1892, 1899, 1900, 1904, 1907, 1908,
1911, 1912, 1914, 1923, 1925, 1927,
1931, 1933, 1937, 1951, 1954, 1965,
1967, 1969, 1971, 1972, 1974, 1975,
1977, 1980, 1985, 1988, 1989, 1995,
2001, 2004, 2005, 2007, 2011, 2012

LEAGUE CUP WINNERS [15 TIMES]

1956/57, 1957/58, 1965/66, 1966/67,
1967/68, 1968/69, 1969/70, 1974/75,
1982/83, 1997/98, 1999/00, 2000/01,
2005/06, 2008/09, 2014/15

EUROPEAN CUP WINNERS 1967

CORONATION CUP WINNERS 1953

MANAGER FACTFILE: RONNY DEILA

D.O.B: 21/09/75

BORN: PORSGRUNN, NORWAY

PLAYING CAREER RECORD:

ODD GRENLAND (1993-2004)

VIKING (2005)

STROMSGODSET (2006-08)

PLAYING HONOURS:

ODD GRENLAND: NORWEGIAN CUP WINNERS (2000)

AS MANAGER:

STROMSGODSET:

NORWEGIAN CUP WINNERS (2010),
NORWEGIAN PREMIER LEAGUE CHAMPIONS (2013)

CELTIC:

LEAGUE CHAMPIONS (2014/15),
LEAGUE CUP WINNERS (2014/15)

NORWEGIAN Ronny Deila was the natural choice to follow Neil Lennon and become the 17th manager of Celtic given his spectacular success at former club Stromsgodset.

After taking the helm at the Drammen-based side in 2008, he quickly transformed the small club's fortunes, guiding them to national cup glory just two years later.

And in 2013, remarkably, he inspired them to their first league championship in 42 years, beating off competition from the established clubs in Norway.

What's more, it was achieved by playing entertaining, attacking, and high-intensity football in a team comprised mostly of talented youngsters. These fantastic feats made him one of the most highly-rated young managers in European football.

A former Norway Under-21 internationalist, Ronny Deila spent his entire playing career in his homeland, making 240 appearances for Odd Grenland over 11 years – where he won the Norwegian Cup – before concluding his career with stints at Viking and Stromsgodset.

A qualified teacher, he is renowned for his progressive, forward-thinking approach and man-management skills.

He has also won acclaim for his ability to develop youngsters into top-class players, including current Celtic midfielder Stefan Johansen, who has flourished in Paradise since his arrival at the start of 2014.

These attributes have seen him compared to Borussia Dortmund coach Jurgen Klopp, someone the Norwegian has huge admiration for and who he has spent time studying his methods with.

All this hadn't gone unnoticed in Paradise, and once Neil Lennon announced he was departing the club at the end of the 2013/14 season, the 38-year-old was immediately identified as the perfect candidate to take the club forward.

On June 6, 2014, Ronny Deila was confirmed as Celtic manager and immediately spoke of his determination to deliver attacking, exciting and attractive football to the Hoops faithful and, ultimately, win further silverware for the Scottish Champions.

It was the start of a new journey in Paradise as the new Hoops boss aimed to continue the club's dominance of the domestic game – and do it in the Celtic Way.

And he did just that in some particular style by leading the Celts to their fourth title in a row and adding the League Cup for good measure.

JULY/AUGUST

THU 3rd	FK KRASNODAR	FRIENDLY	N	3-1	STOKES (3), JOHANSEN (38), McGREGOR (49)
SUN 6th	RAPID VIENNA	FRIENDLY	A	1-1	PUKKI (71)
TUE 8th	LASK LINZ	FRIENDLY	A	5-2	PUKKI (35) (48) (67), BALDE (78), GRIFFITHS (88)
FRI 11th	DUKLA PRAGUE	FRIENDLY	N	0-0	
TUE 15th	KR REYKJAVIK	UEFA CL	A	1-0	McGREGOR (83)
SAT 19th	DYNAMO DRESDEN	FRIENDLY	A	1-1	COMMONS (8)
TUE 22nd	KR REYKJAVIK	UEFA CL	H	4-0	VAN DIJK (13) (20), PUKKI (27) (71)
SAT 26th	ST PAULI	FRIENDLY	A	0-1	
WED 30th	LEGIA WARSAW	UEFA CL	A	1-4	McGREGOR (7)

Similar to the previous season, Celtic kicked off their UEFA Champions League exploits in July following a pre-season jaunt to Austria where new manager, Ronny Deila, ran the rule over the players.

KR Reykjavik and Legia Warsaw were the opponents with the second leg of the Legia game rolling over into August. Fielding an ineligible player saw the Polish side out despite winning both legs.

However, the Celtic's league campaign began on a more familiar footing with a 3-0 midweek win over St Johnstone in Perth before, thanks to the

Commonwealth Games and 'home' Euro ties played at Murrayfield, the Hoops played their first game at Celtic Park.

Dundee United were the visitors on flag day when Fergus McCann raised the colours, and a sparkling performance produced a 6-1 win, but when away trips to Inverness and Dens Park produced a 1-0 defeat and a 1-1 draw, there were signs that Celtic weren't going to have it all their own way.

The Celts also lost out to NK Maribor in the Champions League, but moved into the Europa League.

MONTH'S MAGIC MOMENT

THE BHOYS ARE BACK IN TOWN

The Hoops' return to Celtic Park, following the games being played through in the capital at Murrayfield, was a day to look forward to and it could hardly have turned out any better.

The Celts certainly weren't flagging after Fergus McCann unfurled the green and white standard as it took Jason Denayer only four minutes to score his debut goal in that resounding 6-1 win over Dundee United.

SAT 2nd	TOTTENHAM HOTSPUR	FRIENDLY	N	1-6	LINDSAY (45)
WED 6th	LEGIA WARSAW	UEFA CL	H	3-0	CELTIC AWARDED 3-0 WIN AFTER 2-0 DEFEAT OVERTURNED
WED 13th	ST JOHNSTONE	SPFL	A	3-0	STOKES (55), BITTON (76), McGREGOR (85)
SAT 16th	DUNDEE UNITED	SPFL	H	6-1	DENAYER (4), COMMONS (28), JOHANSEN (34), MULGREW (54), BERGET (62) (90)
WED 20th	NK MARIBOR	UEFA CL	A	1-1	McGREGOR (6)
SAT 23rd	INVERNESS CT	SPFL	A	0-1	
TUE 26th	NK MARIBOR	UEFA CL	H	0-1	
SUN 31st	DUNDEE	SPFL	A	1-1	GRIFFITHS (55)

SEPTEMBER

WED 3rd	VILLARREAL	CHARITY MATCH	A	2-4	KAYAL (26), BERGET (36)
SAT 13th	ABERDEEN	SPFL	H	2-1	DENAYER (6), COMMONS (46)
THU 18th	FC SALZBURG	UEFA EL	A	2-2	WAKASO (14), BROWN (60)
SUN 21st	MOTHERWELL	SPFL	H	1-1	COMMONS (68)
WED 24th	HEARTS	LEAGUE CUP	H	3-0	GUIDETTI (23), COMMONS (56), ECKERSLEY og (60)
SAT 27th	ST MIRREN	SPFL	A	2-1	GUIDETTI (42), (63)

MONTH'S MAGIC MOMENT

THE X-MAN COMETH

Charity was the winner when Hoops legend Paul McStay's Maestros took on Rio Ferdinand's All-Stars in the Maestrio match at Celtic Park.

The Celts won 3-2 with goals from Frank McAvennie and John Hartson sandwiching a dream moment for Celtic-daft Hollywood star James McAvoy, who found the net on the big stage at Paradise.

At the start of August, Inverness Caley Thistle topped the table with 13 points while Celtic, who had played a game fewer, sat in fifth place with seven points while Aberdeen were a place below on six.

The Hoops kicked off with a game against the Dons and drew first blood by recording a 2-1 win that would prove crucial as the campaign progressed. Celtic moved up to fourth while the Pittodrie side slipped to ninth.

However, the momentum was not maintained in the next game as it took a Kris Commons penalty to salvage a draw against Motherwell at Fir Park.

That came following a 2-2 draw with Salzburg in the Europa League, and there was also midweek action following the Lanarkshire trip when the Celts welcomed Hearts on League Cup duty and took the first steps to Hampden with a 3-0 win over the capital side.

That left a trip to Paisley for the last game of the month and a John Guidetti double sealed a 2-1 win for the Hoops over St Mirren.

OCTOBER

October started with more Europa League group stage action as Dynamo Zagreb were beaten 1-0 at Celtic Park, and three weeks later it was Astra Giurgiu's turn to visit Glasgow. This time a 2-1 victory was recorded by the Hoops.

In between those games there was the bread and butter of the SPFL, but Celtic's slice fell butter-down when a 1-0 scoreline gave Hamilton Accies their first win at Celtic Park since 1938.

After the game, the Lanarkshire side topped the table on 20 points while Celtic languished in sixth place with 14.

Some ground was made up in the following game with a comprehensive 5-0 away victory over Ross County and the SPFL card for the month finished with a 2-0 win over Kilmarnock at Celtic Park.

There was one more game to go, and another clinical display saw the Hoops defeat Partick Thistle 6-0 in the League Cup.

MONTH'S MAGIC MOMENT

SIX-SHOOTERS

Celtic hadn't been doing too well in the League Cup in recent years, but things were beginning to look up following on from the previous month's 3-0 win over Hearts.

There was no slip-up when Partick Thistle visited Celtic Park and a John Guidetti hat-trick helped the Celts on their way to a 6-0 win.

					COMMONS (6)
THU 2nd	DINAMO ZAGREB	UEFA EL	H	1-0	
SUN 5th	HAMILTON ACCIES	SPFL	H	0-1	
SAT 18th	ROSS COUNTY	SPFL	A	5-0	GUIDETTI (10), McGREGOR (13), STOKES (29) (56), DENAYER (35)
THU 23rd	FC ASTRA	UEFA EL	H	2-1	SCEPOVIC (72), JOHANSEN (77)
SUN 26th	KILMARNOCK	SPFL	H	2-0	GUIDETTI (35), SCEPOVIC (63)
WED 29th	PARTICK THISTLE	LEAGUE CUP	H	6-0	GUIDETTI (30) (52) (56), IZAGUIRRE (48), GRIFFITHS (62) (68)

NOVEMBER

Once more there were only three SPFL games played by Celtic this month amid cup duty on both European and domestic fronts. The month started with a 1-0 home win over Inverness Caley Thistle that edged the Celts from fourth place to third with a game in hand over every other team in the top six.

The next league meeting was crucial, and on a difficult away trip to Pittodrie when the Hoops went behind, drew level and then had skipper Scott Brown sent off, the 10-man Celtic side were only minutes away from dropping valuable points when Virgil van Dijk turned up at the back post to touch the ball into the net following a corner.

The winning goal was still celebrated in the aftermath of the match and the seeds of the Ronny Roar were planted. The result took Celtic to the top of the table for the first time when they could so easily have been knocked back into fifth place.

The next game saw Dundee defeated 2-1 as Celtic maintained their presence at the top of the table and the month finished with a trip to Tynecastle on Scottish Cup duty where the Hoops recorded a 4-0 win over Hearts.

MONTH'S MAGIC MOMENT

GRANITE-CITY GRIT

No doubt about it - the battling display by 10 men culminating in Virgil van Dijk's last-gasp goal being not only the match winner, but also the turning point in Celtic's season.

Making it to the top of the league for the first time in November went a long way to ensuring that Celts were there in May when it really mattered.

SAT 1st	INVERNESS CT	SPFL	H	1-0		GUIDETTI (48)
THU 6th	FC ASTRA	UEFA EL	A	1-1		JOHANSEN (32)
SUN 9th	ABERDEEN	SPFL	A	2-1		JOHANSEN (37), VAN DIJK (90)
SAT 22nd	DUNDEE	SPFL	H	2-1		STOKES (44), GUIDETTI (54)
THU 27th	FC SALZBURG	UEFA EL	H	1-3		JOHANSEN (30)
SUN 30th	HEARTS	SCOTTISH CUP	A	4-0		VAN DIJK (28) & (61), GUIDETTI (52), STOKES (54)

21

5

DECEMBER

This was a busy month with five SPFL games on the cards but there were fluctuating results as, after three straight wins, points were dropped to Dundee United and Ross County.

First up were Partick Thistle at Celtic Park in midweek and that was closely followed by a trip to Fir Park to take on Motherwell. Both games were won 1-0 as the Hoops, finally on the same games played as the rest of the league, moved three points ahead at the summit.

The following weekend it was St Mirren's turn to visit Celtic Park and the Hoops harvested a 4-1 win, but that was followed by a 2-1 defeat at Tannadice to Dundee United.

The home side's second goal was scored by Stuart Armstrong, but that would be the last domestic goal scored against Celtic until St Johnstone managed it in a 2-1 Hoops win on February 14, and by that time Armstrong had already scored for Celtic.

Celtic's calendar year finished with a dull 0-0 home draw with Ross County.

On the European front, despite losing 4-3 away to Dynamo Zagreb, the Celts had already qualified from Group D for the knockout stages of the Europa League.

MONTH'S MAGIC MOMENT

TOP OF THE TREE

All in all, it wasn't a bad Christmas for those of a green and white persuasion, as the Hoops sat at the top of the table and had guaranteed European football after the festivities.

And, despite not taking full honours from the final two games, the Celts had amassed enough points to still sit at the league summit when the bells rang in the New Year.

WED 3rd	PARTICK THISTLE	SPFL	H	1-0	VAN DIJK (60
SAT 6th	MOTHERWELL	SPFL	A	1-0	STOKES (6)
THU 11th	DINAMO ZAGREB	UEFA EL	A	3-4	COMMONS (23), SCEPOVIC (29), PIVARIC og (81)
SUN 14th	ST MIRREN	SPFL	H	4-1	BROWN (4), (18), FORREST (15), STOKES (67)
SUN 21st	DUNDEE UNITED	SPFL	A	1-2	GRIFFITHS (87)
SAT 27th	ROSS COUNTY	SPFL	H	0-0	

					IZAGUIRRE (36), SCEPOVIC (72)		
MON 5th	KILMARNOCK	SPFL	A	2-0			
SAT 10th	PSV EINDHOVEN	FRIENDLY	N	0-1	GRIFFITHS (1), THOMSON (2)		
TUE 13th	SPARTA PRAGUE	FRIENDLY	N	2-3	MATTHEWS (33), HENDERSON (50)		
SAT 17th	HAMILTON ACCIES	SPFL	A	2-0	VAN DIJK (25), GRIFFITHS (42), LUSTIG (75), (80)		
WED 21st	MOTHERWELL	SPFL	H	4-0	COMMONS (51)		
SAT 24th	ROSS COUNTY	SPFL	A	1-0			

JANUARY

Celtic saw in the New Year at the top of the table, just two points ahead of Aberdeen. But by the time the Hoops played their first game of the New Year, the Dons had played another two games and were now four points ahead.

Celtic pulled three back with a 2-0 away win over Kilmarnock, the first of four games in which the Hoops could concentrate solely on the SPFL (apart from the rejuvenating break in Gran Canaria that is).

When Celtic returned to action with a 2-0 win over Hamilton Accies, they were still two points behind Aberdeen but with two games in hand.

A Wednesday 4-0 rout of Motherwell saw the Hoops move a point ahead at the top, while on Friday Aberdeen could only draw with St Johnstone. On Saturday, a 1-0 win over Ross County put Celtic three points ahead and they still had a game in hand.

MONTH'S MAGIC MOMENT

WELL ON THE WAY

The midweek 4-0 defeat of Motherwell added to the feel-good factor and ensured that Celtic's bid for four-in-a-row was coasting along nicely.

The high point of the night was a wonderfully worked team goal that ended with a diving header from Mikael Lustig.

SUN 1st	RANGERS	LEAGUE CUP	N	2-0	GRIFFITHS (10), COMMONS (31)	
SAT 7th	DUNDEE	SCOTTISH CUP	A	2-0	GRIFFITHS (6), JOHANSEN (46)	
WED 11th	PARTICK THISTLE	SPFL	A	3-0	MACKAY-STEVEN (1), ARMSTRONG (30), JOHANSEN (66)	
SAT 14th	ST JOHNSTONE	SPFL	A	2-1	GRIFFITHS (1), JOHANSEN (52)	
THU 19th	INTER MILAN	UEFA EL	H	3-3	ARMSTRONG (24), CAMPAGNARO og (25), GUIDETTI (90)	
SUN 22nd	HAMILTON ACCIES	SPFL	H	4-0	COMMONS (56), (82), JOHANSEN (64), GUIDETTI (78)	
THU 26th	INTER MILAN	UEFA EL	A	0-1		

FEBRUARY

February was just like the old days, with the Hoops meeting Inter Milan in Europe. But the month started with a derby in the League Cup semi-final that was won 2-0 thanks to goals from Leigh Griffiths and Kris Commons.

That was followed by a Scottish Cup win over Dundee, but amid all the cup action in three different competitions, there were still three SPFL games played.

The first league game finally presented the option of fielding transfer-window signings Gary Mackay-Steven and Stuart Armstrong who had been cup-tied with Dundee United.

They both got off to a flier by scoring in the 3-0 win over Partick Thistle that more or less discounted Aberdeen's 4-0 win over Ross County at the weekend while Celtic were on cup duty.

Both sides won again the following weekend, as they did a week later, meaning that once more Celtic finished the month still three points ahead and still with a game in hand. But that final weekend's card spilled over into Sunday, March 1 when the top two clashed in the East End of Glasgow.

MONTH'S MAGIC MOMENT

HAMPDEN DOUBLE DATE

The eyes of the world were upon the National Stadium for the derby clash in the semi-final of the League Cup and the Hoops came up with the goods.

First-half goals from Leigh Griffiths and Kris Commons set Celtic on their way to the final and gave them a bite at the first silverware of the season.

MARCH

And so the February/March weekend card continued with the Dons intent on levelling with the Celts at the top of the table. But a comprehensive 4-0 victory for the Hoops eased them ahead by six points with that game still in hand.

However, any hope of going nine points ahead were quashed by a wonder-goal from Danny Swanson, who gave St Johnstone an unexpected 1-0 midweek win at Celtic Park.

Aberdeen also clawed back another three points while Celtic were on League Cup duty, but as far as the rest of the month was concerned it was all about Dundee United for the Hoops.

A draw in the Scottish Cup ensured that the teams would meet in four consecutive games in three competitions at three different grounds.

The second game saw Celtic victorious in the League Cup final, while the Scottish Cup replay was also won.

That left the league meeting, and a 3-0 win at Celtic Park on the same day as the Dons drew with Dundee saw the Hoops five points ahead with a game in hand.

MONTH'S MAGIC MOMENT

SILVER SERVICE

Ronny Deila's first chance of winning silverware with the Hoops proved successful as the Celts claimed the League Cup at Hampden.

Strikes from Kris Commons and James Forrest tied up the trophy and ensured it was adorned with green and white ribbons.

		SPFL	H	4-0	DENAYER (37), GRIFFITHS (63), MACKAY-STEVEN (69), JOHANSEN (80)
SAT 1st	ABERDEEN	SPFL	H	0-1	GRIFFITHS (71)
WED 4th	ST JOHNSTONE	SCOTTISH CUP	A	1-1	COMMONS (28), FORREST (78)
SUN 8th	DUNDEE UNITED	LEAGUE CUP	N	2-0	DENAYER (16), GRIFFITHS (57), COMMONS (79), VAN DIJK (90)
SUN 15th	DUNDEE UNITED	SCOTTISH CUP	H	4-0	MACKAY-STEVEN (16), GUIDETTI (33), DENAYER (45)
WED 18th	DUNDEE UNITED				
SAT 21st	DUNDEE UNITED	SPFL	H	3-0	

APRIL

The big talking point of the month was probably the Scottish Cup semi-final against Inverness CT, but the Hoops also managed to cram in six SPFL games and took 16 points from a possible 18.

And the first of those wins came 24 hours before Aberdeen drew with Partick Thistle, however that was nullified two games later when the Pittodrie side beat Kilmarnock the day after the Hoops drew with Inverness CT.

That left Celtic still five points ahead with a game in hand, but two consecutive midweek wins for the Hoops that sandwiched a Saturday 1-0 win for the Dons over Dundee United had the Bhoys eight points ahead, with both teams on 33 games played.

With both teams winning their final game of the month, that eight-point gap stood going into the final month of the season.

MONTH'S MAGIC MOMENT

NOT YOU AGAIN

After playing Dundee United four times consecutively in March, the Hoops only met the Tannadice side once in April, but it did come between two games against Dundee.

However, against United on Tayside, a hat-trick from Leigh Griffiths kept Celtic well on course for the title.

FRI 3rd	ST MIRREN	SPFL	A	2-0	FORREST (63), JOHANSEN (79)
WED 8th	PARTICK THISTLE	SPFL	H	2-0	COMMONS (45), JOHANSEN (62)
SAT 11th	INVERNESS CT	SPFL	A	1-1	GRIFFITHS (3)
WED 15th	KILMARNOCK	SPFL	H	4-1	COMMONS (58), GRIFFITHS (66), (80), (85)
SUN 19th	INVERNESS CT	SCOTTISH CUP	N	2-3 (AET)	VAN DIJK (18), GUIDETTI (103)
WED 22nd	DUNDEE	SPFL	A	2-1	MACKAY-STEVEN (32), VAN DIJK (64)
SUN 26th	DUNDEE UNITED	SPFL	A	3-0	GRIFFITHS (47), (65), (84)

MAY

FRI 1st	DUNDEE	SPFL	H	5-0	GRIFFITHS (30), BROWN (37), COMMONS (72), FORREST (77), BITTON (89)
SUN 10th	ABERDEEN	SPFL	A	1-0	BROWN (49)
FRI 15th	ST JOHNSTONE	SPFL	A	0-0	
SUN 24th	INVERNESS CT	SPFL	H	5-0	SCEPOVIC (5), JOHANSEN (18), SCEPOVIC (70), GRIFFITHS (80), COMMONS (89)

That eight-point gap increased to 11 when Friday night fever gripped Celtic Park as Dundee were soundly beaten by a rampant Hoops. It meant Celtic would only have to draw the following weekend at Pittodrie to claim the title for a fourth successive season.

Or that's what everyone thought as there was the small matter of Aberdeen's visit to Tannadice the afternoon following Celtic's 5-0 win, but Dundee United didn't read the script.

A goal from Robbie Muirhead gave the Tayside club a 1-0 win, and Celtic claimed the title without kicking a ball as Aberdeen dropped from the race.

So it was party time win, lose, or draw at Pittodrie

the following weekend and skipper Scott Brown made sure the party was in full swing for all the right reasons when he started, and finished, the move that delivered the only goal of the game.

That left the penultimate game of the campaign and a match at McDiarmid Park that could've, and probably should've, finished about 5-5, ended 0-0.

There were goals aplenty, however, on Trophy Day when the Hoops crushed Inverness CT 5-0 with a scintillating display of football befitting the occasion.

MONTH'S MAGIC MOMENT

PARTY IN PARADISE

We all knew that we were going to be celebrating, no matter what, on Trophy Day but it would be great to go out on a high with a win.

The Celts duly obliged with one of their best performances of the season, and crushed Inverness CT 5-0 in some style to get the title party going with a bang.

A DAY IN THE LIFE OF A CELTIC CAPTAIN

THE CELTIC FOOTBALL CLUB 1888

TRAINING DAY

GETTING up and going to work is something most of us have to do every day. It's monotonous, often tedious and normally hard to do, but it's a routine nonetheless and something we all have to go through at some point in our lives.

Footballers are no different. Despite the lavish lifestyles they may seem to lead, they too need to get up at the right time, head in to the office and clock in before the boss arrives.

At Celtic it is Hoops captain Scott Brown who sets the rules for getting to Lennoxtown on time, with fines for any player who fails to arrive at his desk before the curfew. However, just how does the skipper make his way to work in the morning?

Well, as chance would have it, the midfielder gave us an insight into his daily routine on an average day of training and, as you may expect, it's surprisingly normal.

8AM: LEAVING THE HOUSE

"I leave Edinburgh at about 8am and come in with the car. I pick up Leigh Griffiths and we go to the shops at the top of Barnton (an area in Edinburgh) as there's a wee bakery there and we get some nice proper homemade coffee.

"I go for a latte, double shot, and Griff has a wee cappuccino. I then get a bottle of Lucozade and I'm flying high.

"In the car we have a wee chat about the weather and politics (aye right) and we get in to training about 9.15am. 9.30am is the cut-off time and there's a fine if you're late.

"I get changed as soon as I'm in, which is a good start, put my kit on and then go up and get some breakfast, usually some Special K. I speak to the lads downstairs and sometimes we have a meeting at 10am and go through what we're going to do for the day, like warm-up, boxes, passing, possession and chat about roughly how long the session's going to be.

"I enjoy training. I enjoy running about and working hard."

12.30PM: AFTER TRAINING

"I come in and maybe will go to the gym depending what day it is. I don't do too much there. I usually just work on my core but I don't lift any weights. I do that then head into the bath and lie there for half-an-hour and then have a shower."

1PM ONWARDS:

"After that I go for lunch at Lennoxtown as the food is excellent and then Griff and I get in the car and head home.

"Depending what I've got on I'll probably spend some time with the kids and have a laugh with them. They keep you going and it is hard work but they go to bed about 8pm and then that's me.

"After that I sit and chill out watching telly. I usually catch up on EastEnders but it's off on a Wednesday, so I'm a bit devastated with that."

See pages 38/39 for Scott's matchday in Paradise.

LOCAL HEROES

A FOOTBALL fan's first match as a supporter always sticks in their mind - and it's the same for football players.

Celtic's stars may have made it to the top of the tree when it comes to the beautiful game as players, but they all started by going to watch games from the stands, just like the Hoops fans.

Unlike most of us, however, the Celtic players took their love of football to the next level and went from being punters to professionals after their first taste of action. But where did the likes of Scott Brown, Kris Commons and Tom Rogic get their first football experiences?

They got them everywhere, from the blustery stands of Cowdenbeath in Scotland to the sun-drenched surroundings of the Canberra Cosmos in Australia.

Here we find out where else the Hoops stars got their start in football, starting with Kris Commons.

Kris Commons

I started out at Mansfield Town in Nottinghamshire. I was actually a mascot there and I still have the strip.

Someone sent me a picture of the programme with the teams recently, Mansfield v Scunthorpe, and then on the bottom it said "Mascot: Kristian Commons," so that was nice.

I was mad keen on football when I was younger so my Mum sort of pushed for me to get a shot as a mascot. We got two complimentary tickets for me being a mascot, but my Mum had to sell her ticket because we were that skint we couldn't afford to send me to be a mascot and have both my parents there.

We paid for me to be a mascot but we sold one of the tickets to retrospectively cover that cost. My Mum just wanted me to do it and I got on the pitch.

Mansfield's Field Mill stadium was where we used to have the school finals and local finals and the last time I played there was at Under-11 level and I scored a hat-trick so I have good memories of it.

Fan memories

I went to watch Mansfield Town there once as well. A friend and I paid £3 to get into the all-standing terracing. It was just a normal Saturday and we weren't even intending on going to see the game but because we were in Mansfield town centre we decided to go.

I played more football than I watched as a youngster, however.

From age seven to eight I'd play on a Saturday and Sunday, so if I was allowed to watch *Match of the Day* at night I would, but I was mostly just concentrating on the playing side of things.

My local team

When I was little I played for Junior Reds, which was the Nottingham Forest youth team. I'd go down to the training ground and I was so keen on the players that played for the first team at that time like Teddy Sheringham, Des Walker and Stuart Pearce, who were all big names.

They were a great team at the time. I went on to play for them and it was good playing for them but I later left them to go Derby, their arch rivals, so it didn't go down too well when I left!

First big match

When I was 17 I signed for Stoke City and about two years later they were playing Brentford in a play-off to get into the Championship. I wasn't in the squad or anything but that was the first time I took my partner, Lisa, to a game.

We had just started dating and she asked me what I did for a living. I told her I played football but I think she presumed I meant that I played football with my mates down the park with jackets for goal posts.

I wasn't in the squad but I asked her if she wanted to come and watch my team play at the Millennium Stadium and we got a supporters' bus down. When we got there she couldn't believe it.

Guðjón Þórðarson was the manager at the time and he won us promotion to the First Division, but then Steve Cotterill came in and that pre-season was when I started playing for the first team.

That was probably the biggest game for me.

See pages 42/43 for Tom Rogic and Virgil van Dijk.

SPOT THE DIFFERENCE

THERE are 10 differences in these pictures of Virgil van Dijk in pre-season action. The first one has been circled, but can you spot the rest?

SPOT THE BALL

There are six match balls in this photo of Player of the Year, Stefan Johansen, as he moves forward from midfield. Only one of them is the real one. Can you spot which one it is?

Answers on pages 62/63.

SPFL SEASON 2014/15 QUIZ

1. How many goals did Celtic lose in their 38 matches?
2. In how many games did Celtic score four goals or more?
3. Which Celt made his debut in Celtic's opening SPFL game?
4. Who played the most SPFL games for the Hoops during the season?
5. Which Celt scored the most goals during the league campaign?
6. Who made the most substitute appearances for the club in the SPFL?
7. How many of Celtic's goals were own goals by the opposition?
8. Which Celt scored the last goal of the campaign?
9. Name a player who scored for and against Celtic during the season.
10. Celtic played Dundee United in four consecutive games in the three domestic competitions, but what was the SPFL scoreline?

Answer on page 62/63.

M8 MATES

THE EDINBURGH BHOYS WHO TRAVEL THROUGH TO GLASGOW TOGETHER

WHILE Celtic as a club has its roots firmly planted in Glasgow, the team that plays at Paradise is full of players who hail from all over Scotland and the rest of the world.

Ronny Deila's starting XI is a multicultural mix of footballers, but there is a quartet of those Bhoys who all hail from around the Scottish capital city.

Club captain Scott Brown, Hoops striker Leigh Griffiths and Celtic goalie Craig Gordon all live in Edinburgh and travel to Lennoxtown together on a regular basis. They have been joined by Livingston Bhoy Liam Henderson since he returned from his loan period in Norway.

More often than not, skipper Broony is on driving duty, which puts an interesting slant on the musical soundtrack to the journey and the topics of conversation discussed on the way to work.

And while Happy Hardcore may not be the favourite genre of music for either Griffiths or Gordon, both stars admit that sharing a lift with their captain isn't all bad.

"It's great being part of that group," said Craig Gordon. "It consists of Scott Brown and Leigh Griffiths, two ex-Hibees who, to be honest, didn't have too much to gloat about last season so normally they're quite quiet.

"We share lifts now and again to and from training or at functions, which can be entertaining.

"I've only come back once from a night out with Leigh. It was after the Player of the Year awards where he'd picked up his top goalscorer award. He talked me through a few of the highlights but normally he's just the same after a night out as he is in the morning.

"Normally when I take Leigh back from training he just sits there nice and quiet. He takes a lot of selfies, for some reason, in the front of my car.

"I don't know where they are going or where they end up, but he does like to take pictures of himself. Somewhere there is a cache full of Leigh Griffiths photos. I don't know where that is, nor do I particularly want to find out either. He's definitely not on some secret modelling contract."

The keeper added: "Now and again the Edinburgh rivalry comes up but with Hearts being so far ahead at the top of the league last season there wasn't really much that Leigh or Scott could say.

"Sometimes we chat about games gone past that we've played against each other but it's all fairly good-natured. I've probably got the best record out of the pair of them in derby matches anyway, so they don't bring it up too often.

"Normally Leigh and Scott come in to training from Edinburgh together and sometimes I take Leigh home. We did all drive back together from Inverness the last time, however, which was probably a few too many hours in their presence than I'd normally care for.

"I heard every Happy Hardcore song there is on that trip. There were not a lot of words spoken but there were certainly a lot of banging tunes played."

SUNSHINE FROM LEITH

Being a former Hibs player means Celtic striker and Edinburgh Bhoy Leigh Griffiths enjoys his trips with his captain, Scott Brown, a little more than former Hearts goalie Craig Gordon.

The former Hibee duo played for the capital side at different times but that doesn't stop the pair from winding up their former Jambos rival, even though the shot-stopper shades the bragging rights in terms of results last term.

It's all light-hearted banter, however, and the Hoops hit-man said their journeys together have helped bring the trio closer together as team-mates.

"Me and Broony normally come in together and it's great hanter with the captain," said Griffiths.

"We've always got stuff to talk about and he loves his DAB radio. If the radio's not playing any decent songs he'll just fire on his phone but you need to be very awake to listen to the songs he's got on his phone. He loves rave, '90s dance, Scooter, you name it, he's got it on his phone.

"In the changing room he'll put a bit of R'n'B on, because I don't think some of the foreign boys are too fond of Scooter.

"For the morning run to training I'll go and get the coffees in before he picks me up and maybe even grab him a roll sometimes if he's hungry.

"It is great being from Edinburgh and having that together, but when you come to Celtic everyone's close. There's a great team spirit and we're all as one."

MAZE

Manager Ronny Deila is visiting his homeland in Norway and has to make his way back to Celtic Park.

Can you help him roar his way back to Paradise by finding the proper route through the maze?

Start

Finish

Find out how Ronny gets back to Scotland on pages 62/63.

CROSSWORD

ACROSS
1. The nationality of Tom Rogic. (10)
6. Celtic won the European Cup against this side. (5,5)
8. Where Craig Gordon played in England. (10)
9. The club we signed Kris Commons from. (5,6)
10. The number of times we have won the league. (5,3)

DOWN
2. Our captain. (5,5)
3. Our opponents in last season's League Cup final. (6,6)
4. Ronny Deila also managed this club. (11)
5. Home country of Efe Ambrose. (7)
7. The club's weekly magazine. (6,4)

QUIZ

1. What do Adam Eckersley of Hearts, Dinamo Zagreb's Josip Pivaric and Hugo Campagnaro of Inter Milan have in common?
2. How many times did Celtic play Dundee United last term?
3. Which Celt changed his number from No.26 during the close season?
4. How many Celtic Parks have the club been based at?
5. How many goals did Celtic concede in their League Cup-winning campaign?

Check out the answers on pages 62/63.

PARADISE PROFILES

SCOTT BROWN	NIR BITTON	KIERAN TIERNEY
JAMES FORREST	STEFAN JOHANSEN	DEDRYCK BOYATA
CHARLIE MULGREW	LEIGH GRIFFITHS	SAIDY JANKO
EMILIO IZAGUIRRE	DARNELL FISHER	NADIR CIFTCI
KRIS COMMONS	CALLUM McGREGOR	LOGAN BAILLY
ANTHONY STOKES	LIAM HENDERSON	SCOTT ALLAN
MIKAEL LUSTIG	CRAIG GORDON	TYLER BLACKETT
TOM ROGIC	STUART ARMSTRONG	RYAN CHRISTIE
EFE AMBROSE	GARY MACKAY-STEVEN	JOZO SIMUNOVIC
DERK BOERRIGTER	LEONARDO FASAN	

SCOTT BROWN

POSITION: MIDFIELDER
SQUAD NUMBER: 8
D.O.B: 25/06/85
BORN: HILL O' BEATH, SCOTLAND
HEIGHT: 5'10"
SIGNED: 01/07/07
DEBUT: V KILMARNOCK (H) 0-0 (SPL) 05/08/07
PREVIOUS CLUBS: HIBERNIAN

JAMES FORREST

POSITION: WINGER
SQUAD NUMBER: 49
D.O.B: 07/07/91
BORN: GLASGOW, SCOTLAND
HEIGHT: 5'9"
SIGNED: 30/08/09
DEBUT: V MOTHERWELL (H) 4-0 (SPL) 01/05/10
PREVIOUS CLUBS: CELTIC YOUTH

CHARLIE MULGREW

POSITION: DEFENDER
SQUAD NUMBER: 21
D.O.B: 06/03/86
BORN: GLASGOW, SCOTLAND
HEIGHT: 6'2"
SIGNED: 01/07/10
DEBUT: V SC BRAGA (A) 0-3 (UCL) 28/07/10
PREVIOUS CLUBS: ABERDEEN, SOUTHEND (LOAN), WOLVES, DUNDEE UNITED (LOAN), CELTIC

EMILIO IZAGUIRRE

POSITION: DEFENDER
SQUAD NUMBER: 3
D.O.B: 10/05/86
BORN: TEGUCIGALPA, HONDURAS
HEIGHT: 5'8"
SIGNED: 18/08/11
DEBUT: V MOTHERWELL (A) 1-0 (SPL) 29/08/10
PREVIOUS CLUBS: MOTAGUA

KRIS COMMONS

POSITION: MIDFIELDER
SQUAD NUMBER: 15
D.O.B: 30/08/83
BORN: NOTTINGHAM, ENGLAND
HEIGHT: 5'6"
SIGNED: 27/01/11
DEBUT: V ABERDEEN (H) 4-1 (CIS) 29/01/11
PREVIOUS CLUBS: DERBY COUNTY, NOTTINGHAM FOREST, STOKE CITY

ANTHONY STOKES

POSITION: STRIKER
SQUAD NUMBER: 10
D.O.B: 25/07/88
BORN: DUBLIN, IRELAND
HEIGHT: 5'11"
SIGNED: 31/08/10
DEBUT: V HEARTS (H) 3-0 (SPL) 11/09/11
PREVIOUS CLUBS: HIBERNIAN, CRYSTAL PALACE (LOAN), SHEFFIELD UNITED (LOAN), SUNDERLAND, FALKIRK (LOAN), ARSENAL

MIKAEL LUSTIG

POSITION: RIGHT-BACK
SQUAD NUMBER: 23
D.O.B: 13/12/86
BORN: UMEA, SWEDEN
HEIGHT: 6'2"
SIGNED: 01/01/12
DEBUT: V ABERDEEN (A) 1-1 (SPL) 03/03/12
PREVIOUS CLUBS: ROSENBORG, GIF SUNDSVALL, UMEA, SANDAKERMS SK

TOM ROGIC

POSITION: MIDFIELDER
SQUAD NUMBER: 18
D.O.B: 16/12/92
BORN: GRIFFITH, AUSTRALIA
HEIGHT: 6'2"
SIGNED: 09/01/13
DEBUT: V INVERNESS CALEY THISTLE (A) 3-1, (SPL) 09/02/13
PREVIOUS CLUBS: CENTRAL COAST MARINERS, BELCONNEN UNITED, ANU FC

EFE AMBROSE

POSITION: DEFENDER
SQUAD NUMBER: 4
D.O.B: 18/10/88
BORN: KADUNA, NIGERIA
HEIGHT: 6'3"
SIGNED: 31/08/12
DEBUT: V DUNDEE (H) 2-0 (SPL) 22/09/12
PREVIOUS CLUBS: FC ASHDOD, KADUNA UNITED

DERK BOERRIGTER

POSITION: ATTACKER
SQUAD NUMBER: 11
D.O.B: 16/10/86
BORN: OLDENZAAL, NETHERLANDS
HEIGHT: 6'4"
SIGNED: 30/06/13
DEBUT: V ROSS COUNTY (H) 2-1 (SPFL) 03/09/13
PREVIOUS CLUBS: AJAX, HAARLEM (LOAN),
ZWOLLE, RKC WAALWIJK, AJAX

NIR BITTON

POSITION: MIDFIELDER
SQUAD NUMBER: 6
D.O.B: 30/10/91
BORN: ASHDOD, ISRAEL
HEIGHT: 6'5"
SIGNED: 30/08/13
DEBUT: V AC MILAN (A) 0-2 (UCL) 18/09/13
PREVIOUS CLUBS: FC ASHDOD

PARADISE PROFILES

STEFAN JOHANSEN

POSITION: MIDFIELDER
SQUAD NUMBER: 25
D.O.B: 08/01/91
BORN: VARDO, NORWAY
HEIGHT: 5'11"
SIGNED: 15/01/14
DEBUT: V HIBERNIAN (A) 4-0 (SPFL) 26/01/14
PREVIOUS CLUBS: STROMSGODSET, BODO/GLIMT

LEIGH GRIFFITHS

POSITION: ATTACKER
SQUAD NUMBER: 9
D.O.B: 20/08/90
BORN: EDINBURGH, SCOTLAND
HEIGHT: 5'8"
SIGNED: 31/01/14
DEBUT: V ABERDEEN (A) 1-2 (SPFL) 08/02/14
PREVIOUS CLUBS: WOLVERHAMPTON WANDERERS,
HIBERNIAN (LOAN), DUNDEE, LIVINGSTON

DARNELL FISHER

POSITION: DEFENDER
SQUAD NUMBER: 41
D.O.B: 04/04/94
BORN: READING, ENGLAND
HEIGHT: 5'9"
DEBUT: V HIBERNIAN (A) 1-1 (SPFL) 19/10/13
PREVIOUS CLUBS: CELTIC YOUTH

CALLUM McGREGOR

POSITION: MIDFIELDER
SQUAD NUMBER: 42
D.O.B: 14/06/93
BORN: GLASGOW, SCOTLAND
HEIGHT: 5'9"
DEBUT: V KR REYKJAVIK (A) 1-0 (UCL) 15/07/14
PREVIOUS CLUBS: CELTIC YOUTH

LIAM HENDERSON

POSITION: MIDFIELDER
SQUAD NUMBER: 53
D.O.B: 25/04/96
BORN: LIVINGSTON, SCOTLAND
HEIGHT: 6'0"
DEBUT: V MOTHERWELL (A) 5-0 (SPFL) 06/12/13
PREVIOUS CLUBS: CELTIC YOUTH

CRAIG GORDON

POSITION: GOALKEEPER
SQUAD NUMBER: 1
D.O.B: 31/12/82
BORN: EDINBURGH, SCOTLAND
HEIGHT: 6'4"
SIGNED: 03/07/14
DEBUT: V ST JOHNSTONE 3-0 (A) (SPFL) 13/08/14
PREVIOUS CLUBS: SUNDERLAND, HEARTS, COWDENBEATH (LOAN)

STUART ARMSTRONG

POSITION: MIDFIELDER
SQUAD NUMBER: 14
D.O.B: 30/03/92
BORN: INVERNESS, SCOTLAND
HEIGHT: 6'0.5"
SIGNED: 02/02/15
DEBUT: V PARTICK THISTLE 3-0 (A) (SPFL) 11/02/15
PREVIOUS CLUBS: INVERNESS CALEY THISTLE, DUNDEE UNITED

GARY MACKAY-STEVEN

POSITION: MIDFIELDER
SQUAD NUMBER: 16
D.O.B: 31/08/90
BORN: THURSO, SCOTLAND
HEIGHT: 5'9"
SIGNED: 02/02/15
DEBUT: V PARTICK THISTLE 3-0 (A) (SPFL) 11/02/15
PREVIOUS CLUBS: AIRDRIE UNITED, DUNDEE UNITED

LEONARDO FASAN

POSITION: GOALKEEPER
SQUAD NUMBER: 38
D.O.B: 04/01/94
BORN: SAN VITO AL TAGLIAMENTO, ITALY
HEIGHT: 6'2"
SIGNED: 01/07/14
DEBUT: N/A
PREVIOUS CLUBS: UDINESE (YOUTH)

KIERAN TIERNEY

POSITION: DEFENDER
SQUAD NUMBER: 63
D.O.B: 05/06/97
BORN: WISHAW, SCOTLAND
HEIGHT: 5'10"
SIGNED: 01/07/13
DEBUT: V DUNDEE 2-1 (A) (SPFL) 22/04/15
PREVIOUS CLUBS: CELTIC YOUTH

DEDRYCK BOYATA

POSITION: DEFENDER
SQUAD NUMBER: 20
D.O.B: 28/11/90
BORN: BRUSSELS, BELGIUM
HEIGHT: 6'2"
SIGNED: 02/06/15
DEBUT: V FC STJARNAN 2-0 (H) (UCL) 15/07/15
PREVIOUS CLUBS: MANCHESTER CITY, BOLTON (LOAN), FC TWENTE (LOAN)

SAIDY JANKO

POSITION: DEFENDER
SQUAD NUMBER: 22
D.O.B: 22/10/1995
BORN: ZURICH, SWITZERLAND
HEIGHT: 5'10"
SIGNED: 01/07/15
DEBUT: V ROSS COUNTY 2-0 (H) (SPFL) 01/08/17
PREVIOUS CLUBS: BOLTON WANDERERS (LOAN), MANCHESTER UNITED, FC ZURICH

NADIR CIFTCI

POSITION: ATTACKER
SQUAD NUMBER: 7
D.O.B: 12/02/92
BORN: KARAKOCAN, TURKEY
HEIGHT: 6' 1"
SIGNED: 09/07/15
DEBUT: V FC STJARNAN 2-0 (H) (UCL) 15/07/15
PREVIOUS CLUBS: PORTSMOUTH, KAYSERISPOR, NAC BREDA, DUNDEE UNITED

SCOTT ALLAN

POSITION: MIDFIELDER
SQUAD NUMBER: 19
D.O.B: 28/11/91
BORN: GLASGOW, SCOTLAND
HEIGHT: 5'7"
SIGNED: 14/08/15
DEBUT: V DUNDEE UNITED 3-1 (A) (SPFL) 22/08/15
PREVIOUS CLUBS: HIBERNIAN, BIRMINGHAM CITY (LOAN), PORTSMOUTH (LOAN), MK DONS (LOAN), PORTSMOUTH (LOAN), WEST BROMWICH ALBION, FORFAR (LOAN), DUNDEE UNITED

LOGAN BAILLY

POSITION: GOALKEEPER
SQUAD NUMBER: 26
D.O.B: 27/12/85
BORN: LIEGE, BELGIUM
HEIGHT: 6' 3"
SIGNED: 08/07/15
DEBUT: V DUNDEE UNITED 3-1 (A) (SPFL) 22/08/15
PREVIOUS CLUBS: GENK, HEUSDEN-ZOLDER (LOAN), BORUSSIA MUNCHENGLADBACH, NEUCHATEL XAMAX (LOAN), GENK (LOAN), OH LEUVEN

TYLER BLACKETT

POSITION: DEFENDER
SQUAD NUMBER: 2
D.O.B: 02/04/94
BORN: MANCHESTER, ENGLAND
HEIGHT: 6'2"
SIGNED: 29/08/15
DEBUT: V N/A
PREVIOUS CLUBS: MANCHESTER UNITED, BIRMINGHAM CITY (LOAN), BLACKPOOL (LOAN)

RYAN CHRISTIE

POSITION: MIDFIELDER
SQUAD NUMBER: 17
D.O.B: 22/02/95
BORN: INVERNESS, SCOTLAND
HEIGHT: 5'10"
SIGNED: 01/09/15
DEBUT: V N/A
PREVIOUS CLUBS: INVERNESS CALEDONIAN THISTLE

JOZO SIMUNOVIC

POSITION: DEFENDER
SQUAD NUMBER: 5
D.O.B: 04/08/94
BORN: ZAGREB, CROATIA
HEIGHT: 6'3"
SIGNED: 01/09/15
DEBUT: V N/A
PREVIOUS CLUBS: DINAMO ZAGREB

CAPTAIN'S DAY

THE CELTIC FOOTBALL CLUB 1888

A DAY IN THE LIFE OF A CELTIC CAPTAIN

MATCH DAY

WHEN it comes to game day there are few better feelings than pulling your scarf on and heading to the match after following your pre-match routine.

For some Hoops supporters that might involve getting up at a decent time to have their traditional pre-match breakfast before jumping on the train or in the car to head to the game.

For others it might be a case of meeting friends down the pub for a few light refreshments before talking a stroll to Paradise to catch the Bhoys in action.

As fans we all have our pre-match rituals but what is it like for the Celtic players?

The routine of a player before and on the day of a game is often shrouded in mystery, but Celtic captain Scott Brown has pulled back the curtain to give us an insight into what happens behind scenes with the Celtic first team.

A lot of eating and a lot of sleeping seems to be the most consistent theme throughout the days before and after a match, but the Celts' captain revealed that there are a few idiosyncrasies unique to the champions.

FROM 6PM: THE DAY BEFORE

"We're in the hotel the night before and we usually meet up at about 6.30pm. Sometimes Leigh Griffiths and I go straight there from training, but if it's on a Saturday we get to go home first without rush hour traffic and see our kids and families.

"If it's a Friday and we're playing on the Saturday we go to the hotel straight from training and get there about 2.30pm or 3pm. The lads come about 6.30pm and we have dinner at 7pm.

"We then have snacks at 9.30pm, but I get a rub from the two masseurs before all that at 5.30pm to 6.45pm. After snacks we chill out, see the lads and have a bit of banter then it's time for bed."

9AM: GAME DAY

"If it's a 3pm kick-off the next day I'll usually go down for breakfast at the hotel on game day. If it's an early kick-off then no one makes breakfast, because there's no point eating breakfast and the pre-match meal at the same time.

"If it's a 3pm kick-off, pre-match is at 11.30am or 11.45am by the time we have our meetings. After that we go for a walk around the hotel for 15 minutes as it's good to go out and get some fresh air."

12NOON: PRE-MATCH

"I have cereal, toast and eggs for pre-match with a couple of bottles of water, and when that's done and dusted we go for the bus and have a bit craic with the lads.

"I check the music collection and make sure everything's half decent for the lads once we get into the changing room. I've got a wee playlist so I go on that and change it up.

"A few of the lads have decent music so they get that on and I just push play in the changing room."

1PM-1.30PM: ARRIVAL

"From arriving at the stadium to heading out for warm up I just focus on the game.

"I speak to Kendo (John Kennedy) about set-plays and then I go and get my ankles strapped. I've had problems in the past so I always make sure they're strapped heavily for the games.

"I get my kit on but I don't have a rub or anything before a game. Someone reads the questions at the back of the official programme and usually me, Charlie Mulgrew and wee Griff try to answer them.

"Then we get changed and we're quite quick to be fair. We need to be in at the stadium an hour-and-a-half before kick-off so it's good just to have that wee chill-out time."

2.55PM: TUNNEL, HUDDLE, KICK-OFF

"I never plan what I say in the Huddle. It's just whatever comes to my head and hopefully it's good.

"It seems to have worked in recent seasons."

4.45PM ONWARDS: POST-MATCH

"Post-match we get pizza right after the game to get some carbohydrates back into the body and get the muscles working. We get a protein shake as well to help repair our muscles and then I lie in the bath for 20 minutes again and that's why I'm always last out!

"It's a nice hot bath to relax my muscles. It seems to have worked for me for the last 13 years. I just do the things I know that work and I don't get any aches or pains when I wake up in the morning.

"I still have to do post-match press conferences sometimes. It can be frustrating when it's a situation like the Scottish Cup semi-final against Inverness last season and you've not seen the incident which makes it hard.

"On a good day it's fine, however, and when it's for our fans I enjoy it. There are no worries whatsoever. Sometimes you just have to be short and sharp on other occasions but, to be fair, I think I say the same things every time."

See pages 50/51 for Scott's away-day schedule.

WELCOME TO 'RONNY' SCOTLAND

RONNY DEILA arrived as Celtic manager in June 2014, and it didn't take him very long to get settled into life in and around Glasgow. Here, he gives his impressions of life in Glasgow and Scotland, and tells us how he relaxes away from football.

GLASGOW

I was here for the Barcelona game back in 2012, but apart from that I was in Scotland once before. It was about 15 years ago and we went to see Rangers play Dunfermline. We had friends who would go all over the world, and at that time they went to Glasgow where Rangers had a home-game, so we went to see them play. Glasgow for me is a very nice city. I enjoy being here and the people are always very nice. Even during the hard period early in the season, not one person came up to me and said anything negative. They were all very supportive. That was unbelievable to hear.

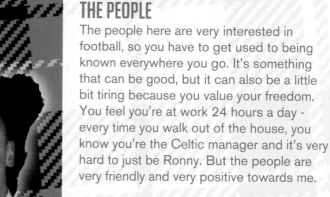

THE PEOPLE

The people here are very interested in football, so you have to get used to being known everywhere you go. It's something that can be good, but it can also be a little bit tiring because you value your freedom. You feel you're at work 24 hours a day - every time you walk out of the house, you know you're the Celtic manager and it's very hard to just be Ronny. But the people are very friendly and very positive towards me.

OUT AND ABOUT

The city is very nice. There are a lot of opportunities if you want – nice restaurants, different restaurants – the cultural life is very good. There is always something you can do. There's nothing that you'd want to do that isn't in Glasgow… maybe apart from staying on the beach, but that's a thing for the whole of northern Europe.

MY FAMILY

They have been overwhelmed. They're proud – of course they're proud – but also worried because they can see the pressure in this job and the amount of tension involved in it – for a mother, it's hard to see. But my mother and father live a Celtic life now as well. They watch every game, they have friends who do the same, so their living room is full when Celtic are playing – it's fantastic. They hurt when Celtic lose, the same way that I hurt when we lose, and they're happy when I'm happy.

RELAXING

One thing I've found that's important to me is sleep. If I don't sleep, it's the worst thing for my body. I have to laugh. I'm a very sociable guy, so I go out and I enjoy being sociable – going for dinner, I enjoy music and the cultural life – but, again, it has to be done in the right moments and the right time. I also have to take care that I get the sleep that I need, so there's a lot of planning.

MUSIC

I listen to all kinds of music, but I like calm music. I don't really listen to the lyrics, I prefer the melody. I love listening to voices. But I like Irish music too. I listen to a lot of Johnny Cash, old music, Elvis. I'm more a 1960s and '70s music than the '80s. I also like *Caledonia* – it's a great song that I can really relate to. When heard the lyrics to that song, I thought - that's almost my life.

LOCAL HEROES

SYDNEY FC

Tom Rogic

I'm from Canberra in Australia but there is no A League team there so the closest team was Sidney FC.

Years back, before the A League, we had a team called the Canberra Cosmos and I remember going to watch a few games there. I went to see them with my family and parents but I must have been really young.

It was strange when I was younger because in Australia there were so many sports competing to be number one, like AFL, Rugby League and Cricket, but in the last five years there has been a big progression. I think it's heading in the right direction so it's exciting for football in Australia at the moment.

Early memories

I naturally grew up playing football with my brother and cousins, and when you see any sort of professional team playing, especially if they are where you're from, it gives you a bit of a lift and helps you want to become professional as well.

I remember watching the national team games on the telly a lot. The big one for me was the Australia v Uruguay match in 2005 to qualify for the 2006 World Cup. It went to penalties and it was the first time Australia qualified for the World Cup in 32 years.

They played home and away, and the home leg was in Sydney and that was the biggest sporting moment I've watched as a kid. That was probably the thing that inspired me most to be a professional footballer.

I must have been 12 or 13 at the time. I was training a lot and getting into the routine of football every day.

KEEPING IT IN THE CELTIC FAMILY

THERE was a family fun day on the afternoon of the SPFL trophy presentation and more than a few Celtic kids celebrated with their Dads who brought the silverware to Paradise.

BEACH BHOYS

At the height of summer there's nothing better than a kick-about on the beach, but who would your Celtic heroes like to face up to by the sea?

Well, we asked them.

ANTHONY STOKES

In our era we have been blessed with amazing talents, but maybe someone like George Best. It would be great to have a kick around with a legend like that and he would also have plenty of stories to tell you to pass the time.

LIAM HENDERSON

I'd maybe say Steven Gerrard. As a midfielder myself I've watched his career and he's just a great footballer. I wouldn't say I've based my game on him, but he's someone I admire as a footballer.

MIKAEL LUSTIG

I only have one idol, Alessandro Del Piero. I've always been a big supporter of him, his passion, being No.10 and he's Italian. I was a big Juventus fan and I loved the way he played. I got to see him play live and that was great, especially when I was younger when I followed the games. When they won and lost you'd almost be crying every time. I'd play alongside him and try to play one-twos.

CRAIG GORDON

I'd need a decent striker. Cristiano Ronaldo I think. His free kicks are very tough to save, so if he was out there with me at least I'd be able to come back with the knowledge of how to save those shots.

KRIS COMMONS

Eric Cantona. He's a legend. I think he used to play a bit of beach football so he might be able to teach me a thing or two.

KIERAN TIERNEY

Well that's easy. Bobo Balde. Ever since I was young he's been my hero and the way he played was just inspirational. I know some of the boys would have other players but I'd be delighted with big Bobo.

COLOURING-IN

We want you to get out your crayons, ink markers or paints and bring this image of Scott Brown and Gary Mackay-Steven to full Celtic technicolour.

GUESS WHO?

1

2

3

4

5

Answers on pages 62/63.

CELTIC FOOTBALL CLUB

BEST AND WORST

IMAGINE you're a Celtic star and you've just moved into a new house. All your furniture and belongings have been moved in and you've just started to find your feet when your new neighbour comes round to introduce themselves. It turns out to be one of your fellow Celtic team-mates, but who do you want it to be?

Who would be the best and who would be the worst to live next to? Whose taste in music or late night antics would make it heaven or hell to live with?

And what if your other new neighbour next door was a celebrity? Who out of the world of television, film or music would you love or loathe to have next door to you and why?

We asked some of the Celtic first-team stars those tricky questions, and their answers may surprise you!

First up is Hoops attacker...

KRIS COMMONS

BROONY'S HOUSE

FORREST'S HOUSE

PLAYER

The best player to live next to would be Broony. He'd always have a house party on a Saturday and we'd be able to play golf every day. That's what I look for in a neighbour.

Our friendship would definitely last through that.

The worst would be James Forrest. He requires a minimum of 16 hours of sleep a day, so he'd constantly be telling us to turn the music down and he also doesn't play golf.

That would impact on the set up Scott Brown and I had going on.

HARMON'S HOUSE

CYRUS' HOUSE

CELEBRITY

That's easy. The best celebrity would be Butch Harmon. He's a golf pundit and he'd hopefully give me a few cheeky lessons.

He taught Tiger Woods when he was younger so he'd be pretty good to have around.

He'd also be good for sliding me a few VIP tickets for backstage access at golf events. That'd be great.

The worst celebrity would be Miley Cyrus. I have a five-year-old girl and I would hate to think that she was looking up to her.

It's not so much her music. If I didn't see her or know about her I'd listen to the music and think, 'Okay, this is not too bad'. She's not a role model that I'd like to see my daughter looking up to.

CHARLIE MULGREW

AMBROSE'S HOUSE

塞尔特

塞尔特

VAUGHAN'S HOUSE

HA! HA! HA!

CELEBRITY

For a famous person I'd go for Vince Vaughan. Every one of his films is hilarious and he's a really funny guy. I think he'd be really funny to live with and I love his movies.

The worst would be that guy Keith Lemon. I don't find him funny at all. I don't think he's a funny guy and I think he'd annoy me if I was living with him next door.

PLAYER

Like Kris, the best player to live next to would be Broony. We're quite similar in a lot of ways and he always has a lot of energy, which I quite like.

We're similar ages and we like to have a laugh and mess about.

The worst player to live next to would be Efe Ambrose. I really like Efe and he's a great guy but he watches Chinese movies at three o'clock in the morning and keeps everybody awake.

I found that out when somebody chapped his room door in Turkey when we went there for a mid-season camp. I could hear a lot of Chinese voices and we knocked on the door and Efe answered.

I know he doesn't speak Chinese, but he watches Chinese movies. I think he's a martial arts fan or something.

LEIGH GRIFFITHS

LEMON'S HOUSE

LOL!

COLLINS' HOUSE

5AM

WAKASO'S HOUSE

SHEERAN'S HOUSE

PLAYER

The best person would have been Mubarak Wakaso for his banter. His one-liners were top notch.

Other than him I'd say James Forrest. He loves a Nando's, so he'd always be inviting me out for lunch and you can't knock that back.

The worst to live next to would be John Collins. He'd always have you out running and doing extra stuff even though you've just finished training. He's always on.

He's always out running and I'm sure he's up at Lennoxtown having a run before the players arrive.

CELEBRITY

Ed Sheeran would be the best celeb to have next door, just so he could sing to me. The guy's voice is a joke, in a good way. He's very good. I went to see him at the Hydro a while back, so I'd bring him back for a few beers or invite him to a game if he lived next to me.

The worst person to live next to would be that Katy Hopkins. She just slaughters people and says horrible things.

CAPTAIN'S DAY

A DAY IN THE LIFE OF A CELTIC CAPTAIN

EURO AWAY GAME

EVER wondered what it was like to travel abroad with the Celtic team for a big European tie?

Well there's one player in the Celtic squad who's done that more than most and that's the captain of the champions, Scott Brown.

The Celts' skipper broke the half-century for European appearances for the club last season, and has travelled abroad with the club so many times that he has developed a strict routine that he sticks to for every Euro trip.

From getting up nice and early to arrive for check-in on time, to having a laugh with the boys on the plane, Hoops captain Broony breaks down exactly what's involved for an away European match for a Celtic player.

LEAVING THE HOUSE:

"I try to get to the airport as early as possible, so we normally have to leave earlier than everyone else because we're coming through from Edinburgh and we hit all the traffic.

It's usually a 9am meet at the airport. Once we get in there I get a nice coffee and chill out in the sky lounge and have a wee bit of banter with the boys, which usually isn't flowing that well at that time in the morning to be fair!"

PLANE DEPARTURE:

"When it's time to fly out you just get on board and relax. You don't think about the match. You don't want to start over-thinking things a day-and-a-half too early as you'll put yourself under a lot of pressure.

So you just chill out, watch a couple of films and have a bit of banter with the lads. If someone falls asleep the standard thing is to steal their trainers or tie their laces together, just the usual guys' banter."

ARRIVAL:

"When we arrive at the hotel after landing we'll have lunch straight away and then get to our rooms. Usually I'll do press with the gaffer and after that we just chill until we get on the pitch at the stadium for an hour the night before the game.

We'll do a bit of warm-up, possession and passing and just try to get used to the surface. People don't realise that every pitch is different so it's important to get used to it.

You just go in, listen to the gaffer, see what he wants from us and then get used to the pitch to see if it's a stud or a mould.

The evening before the game we have our meal and I get a rub for an hour or so after training, then head back to my room for about 10pm. I'll chill out for a bit then get to sleep."

GAME DAY:

"I'll get up about 8am and head down for snacks. I can't sleep too long as I feel rubbish if I do. Others sleep for a lot longer but not me. Usually Stevie Woods and I are up at that time and a few of the young lads as well.

Sometimes we'll head out for a light training session that morning and we'll walk through set-plays or patterns that the manager wants to go over with us. It all depends on how far away the facility is for training.

After that we come back and have a meeting about the game. We'll watch some videos of the team we're playing and see what they're like and see how they play.

After that you go back up to your room. Some people go for another sleep, but I just chill out and watch the TV or another movie.

Three hours and 45 minutes before the game we'll go for a wee walk with Stevie Woods (goalkeeping coach) for 15 minutes. Everyone meets downstairs and we'll get a coffee or a wee juice before we go out with him for a bit.

Then three-and-a-half hours before the game we have a meeting with the gaffer and then three hours and 15 minutes before the match we eat our pre-match meal."

POST-MATCH:

"If it's been a good game then it's brilliant getting back on the bus, especially if we've got three points.

The feeling is amazing and all the lads are chirpy on the bus, talking about the game. You'll be laughing at the lads' bad touches or if anyone had a bad tackle or fell stupidly during the game, just their wee moments.

But if you lose then everyone's quiet and it's forgotten about.

Our flight normally doesn't get back home until 3am or 4am, so the lads are usually quite quiet and they tend to settle down halfway through the flight home.

I've got an hour's drive back to Edinburgh with Leigh Griffiths and Craig Gordon after that, but by the time I get home I'm so tired that I find it quite easy to just go to sleep.

All the adrenaline has gone out your body so you just go straight to bed but then the kids are up two-and-a-half hours later for school, so that's brilliant!"

See pages 60/61 for when Scott puts his feet up.

RAINY DAY MOVIE

THERE'S nothing worse than being stuck in the house when the rain is pelting down, but you can still find plenty to do. We asked a few Celts what DVD they would pop in to pass the time, and here are their answers.

LIAM HENDERSON

No Strings Attached with Natalie Portman and Ashton Kutcher. It's unbelievable, a great film. I think I've seen it a few times already but it never gets old.

MIKEAL LUSTIG

It'd need to be something funny. I'd go for *Old School*. It's one of the best comedies ever

CRAIG GORDON

Cool Runnings. It's funny and it would brighten up my day.

KRIS COMMONS

Cast Away without doubt. It'd be helpful for tips on how to survive if I was on a desert island. I might need to learn how to knock one of my own teeth out.

EOGHAN O'CONNELL

I would probably take *Step Brothers*, it's funny to watch if you are feeling bored. It's not what you want if you are feeling in the mood for a romcom or something but I'll go for it.

KIERAN TIERNEY

Stand By Me. It's a classic film about kids having a tough time of it and I could maybe relate to it a bit.

DOT-TO-DOT

JOIN up all of the dots in this picture and see if you can identify the subjects and the occasion.

Answer on pages 62/63.

THROUGH THE TRANSFER WINDOW

See if you can match up the Celtic player with the club from which he signed

CELTIC

1 EMILIO IZAGUIRRE
2 NIR BITTON
3 SCOTT BROWN
4 STEFAN SCEPOVIC
5 BRIAN McCLAIR
6 GEORGIOS SAMARAS
7 LUBO MORAVCIK
8 PAUL HARTLEY
9 JAN VENNEGOOR OF HESSELINK
10 GARY HOOPER

?

1 DUISBURG
2 SPORTING GIJON
3 SCUNTHORPE UNITED
4 PSV EINDHOVEN
5 MOTAGUA
6 HEARTS
7 MOTHERWELL
8 HIBERNIAN
9 MANCHESTER CITY
10 FC ASHDOD

Answers on pages 62/63.

55

LOCAL HEROES

Scott Brown

My hometown club was Cowdenbeath, the Blue Brazil. I played with them when I was younger and Craig Levein used to come down and take our training sessions.

It was great because he was a young manager just starting out, but he's gone on leaps and bounds since then.

I remember going to the games, but I also remember going to see the stock car racing as well. They raced on the track that surrounded the pitch so the pitch used to get destroyed now and then, which probably helped the style of football! That's where I learned to pass the ball the way I do nowadays.

Early memories

I was a ballboy there when I was younger and I'd get 50p and a pie, it was great. I also used to travel on the bus with my pals and it was always the same bus. It was just the one bus actually, there were so few of us.

We'd go to see Cowdenbeath play Queen's Park at Hampden. I was young at the time but the bus only cost £2. You'd go to games at Hampden and there were only 200 fans inside the ground so that was quite amusing to see.

You'd be able to hear everything all the lads were shouting but if you were at a Scotland game there you wouldn't be able to make out a thing.

Memorable moments

There are more memorable matches for Cowdenbeath now, but not so much when I was supporting them. I think they scored a goal once! That was great.

In recent years they've been doing quite well and they've gone up the leagues so it's all credit to them.

56

Efe Ambrose

I never watched football when I was younger, I just played it. The first club I played for was just with friends when we were kids. We would just go to another neighbourhood and we'd select ourselves and play our best XI against one from another area.

It was a community that brought young talent through. We'd play on this really small pitch or on the road with stones. We'd just keep playing. I had moved to that area when I was six or seven-years-old and I cherish the memories from that time.

Back then football was not that big in Nigeria and most people preferred to go to school rather than play football. It was just fun, not a career.

No one realised it would be able to change your life. It was just something for fun.

First start

After that I got into Campos United, which was in Narayi, Kaduna. That's not far from where I lived. There was a pitch there and they saw the talent in me and I went to what they called Elite level.

I played good matches of a decent standard. There was a coach to give instructions but there was a crisis in the country at that time and the team finished. They changed to Narayi United and I joined them. This all happened when I was eight to 11-years-old. It happened when I was very young.

I didn't stay there for long and after that I went to Kaduna United, which is where I started as a professional footballer.

First big games

I played against each local government in my state. We played for the local government cup and I represented Cagarco. We came second that year and I scored most of the goals in the tournament.

I was not a natural defender at that time and I was on the wing. After that I started developing and seeing the other picture of what football can give you.

You got paid for playing as well as getting a winning bonus with an allowance for food, so I started to see the different side. You could stay away from home and I started moving around with them. Then people started noticing me and I got a move to Kaduna Youth.

I played with them and we came second in the Challenge Cup. We never played the final because there was a fight on the pitch. After that I moved to Kaduna United where I started playing as a professional footballer in 2004.

First professional contract

I played there for two years and got to the Under-23 Olympics team with my country from 2006 to 2008. I played in the all-African games and then I represented my country at the Olympics and we won the silver medal in Beijing in 2008.

This was where I started in centre-half. In my youth I sometimes played in the defence and my coach noticed that I could play there. Anytime there was a need, he asked me to play in the defensive line so I filled in.

Then he started playing me there regularly and said it looked like my position. He told me, football is a crazy job and you might feel that a certain position is your favoured place but it's not really.

He advised me that I could play in the defence, and God can bless me from there and take me anywhere. From there I went to Israel with FC Ashdod and then Europe with Celtic, and I'll stick to his advice.

The most important thing for me is playing and helping the team. Playing in defence allowed me to do that. When I then got to the national team I told them I'd been playing centre-half for a while and the rest is history.

FROM TANNADICE TWINS TO PARADISE PAIR

STEWART ARMSTRONG

MOVING home is a big moment for anyone, but moving job at the same time can be a massive upheaval.

Thankfully for Stuart Armstrong his move from Dundee United to Celtic in January was seamless, and made even easier by having his pal and fellow former team-mate Gary Mackay-Steven join him on that move.

Since then the Tannadice Twins have settled in to their new surroundings nicely and have found their feet in Glasgow.

So whether it's the coffee shops, the parks or the abundance of restaurants to choose from, both players have admitted that they are quite happy now being Glasgow guys rather than Dundee dudes.

MOVING TO GLASGOW

When he was at Dundee United, Andy Robertson once told me that Glasgow was the Big Smoke, and he knew how to handle the Big Smoke and I didn't. But it has been okay, Gaz spent most of his time in Edinburgh so I've had to hold his hand through a few things.

FAVOURITE THING

The variety of restaurants and shops is great. I like going for walks in the West End but there's a lot to do and see so you're never stuck. There's nothing that I don't like about Glasgow really.

LIFE AT CELTIC

It was frantic at the start but now it seems like normal life and I'm getting used to it.

I'm developing, and enjoying football again. After training, Gaz and I like to go for coffees or a smoothie, or even a green tea sometimes. Anything you can imagine, we've been there.

FAVOURITE CELTIC SONG

The one the boys all like is the Efe Ambrose *Ballon d'Or* song, and I think Efe likes that too, but the fans sing so many it's hard to chose.

My favourite one was when we were doing the Huddle before the Inter Milan game and they were singing *You'll Never Walk Alone*. I loved that.

BEST CELTIC MEMORY

My favourite memory so far was scoring against Inter Milan. It was such a big night, such a big occasion and was great to score on my European debut for the club.

BEST THING ABOUT GLASGOW

The shops, restaurants, and the choice of coffee shops where we stay are great. We live next to Kelvingrove Park as well and that's great on a nice day.

MISS ANYTHING ABOUT DUNDEE?

I miss my flat perhaps in Dundee as I lived on the water and had a great view but everything else in Glasgow kind of trumps it.

LIFE AT CELTIC

Life at Celtic is great and I enjoy the training and games. Every game is big because no matter who you're playing, they'd love to beat you and they try to do that.

The support is unbelievable, which is nice at all the games, and I've really been made to feel welcome here.

FAVOURITE CELTIC SONG

I haven't picked out a favourite song yet, but it's something I've been meaning to do. I like the song the fans sing about Efe Ambrose. That's funny every time, and I know he likes it too.

I think I'll get the chords for the Efe one and play that on the guitar one day for the boys.

BEST PLACE FOR ENTERTAINMENT

I've been to a few concerts at the Hydro and that's quite close by. I saw Usher and Ben Howard in there and I've been enjoying going there anytime there's a show on.

FAVOURITE CELTIC MEMORY

My favourite Celtic memory so far was the Inter Milan game. I enjoyed my debut of course but experiencing that atmosphere in the park was special and that's what football is all about really.

GARY MACKAY-STEVEN

Now as the pair head into the Christmas of their first full season at the Bhoys, Mackay-Steven explained just what it was like to shift clubs and cities in the one go.

MOVING TO GLASGOW

It's a little bit bigger than Dundee and there are more attractions here for sure. It was a change but I love it and it's a great place to be.

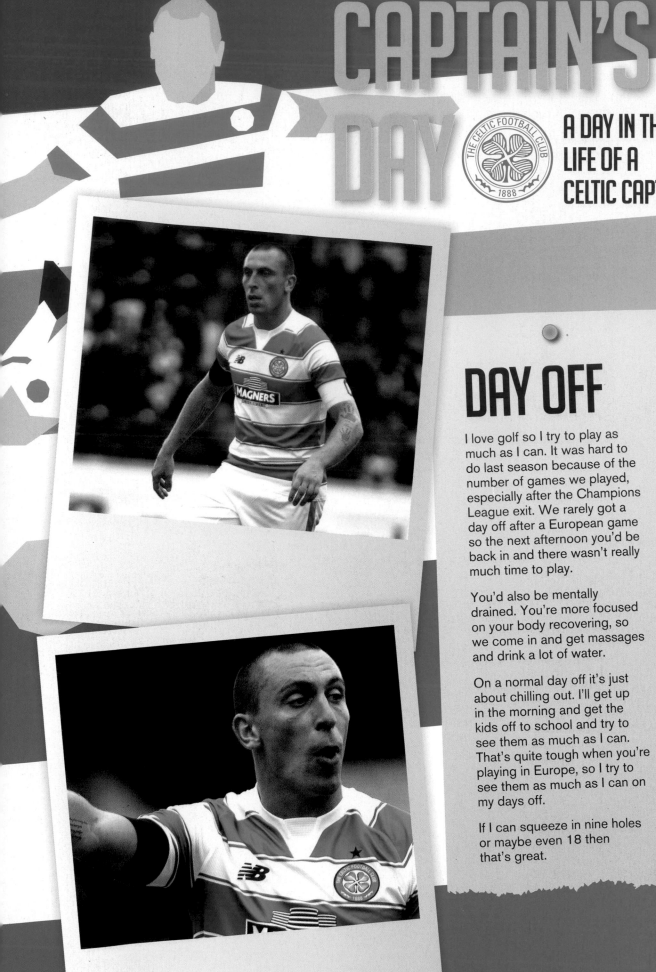

A DAY IN THE LIFE OF A CELTIC CAPTAIN

THE CELTIC FOOTBALL CLUB 1888

MAGNERS

DAY OFF

I love golf so I try to play as much as I can. It was hard to do last season because of the number of games we played, especially after the Champions League exit. We rarely got a day off after a European game so the next afternoon you'd be back in and there wasn't really much time to play.

You'd also be mentally drained. You're more focused on your body recovering, so we come in and get massages and drink a lot of water.

On a normal day off it's just about chilling out. I'll get up in the morning and get the kids off to school and try to see them as much as I can. That's quite tough when you're playing in Europe, so I try to see them as much as I can on my days off.

If I can squeeze in nine holes or maybe even 18 then that's great.

FREEDOM TO ROAM

There's a little bit more freedom for me living in Edinburgh rather than Glasgow. There's a big difference to be perfectly honest.

When I go through to Glasgow to meet the lads or go for a coffee you notice everyone looking and staring at you. In Edinburgh you're not noticed as much so it is easier to just go to the shops or go for dinner with your mates.

It's a bit easier and it's better for me to stay out of the "goldfish bowl."

I stay down at Cramond so it's great to just take the dogs down the beach for a walk. I've got two Labradors and two kids so it's hard work but I've got a lot of energy.

The kids enjoy being outdoors as well, and after we've been out and about I'll come home and we'll usually go for dinner. That's about it really. It's all about relaxing.

ANSWERS

SPOT THE BALL

PAGE 26 - MAZE

PAGE 23 - SPFL SEASON 2014-15 QUIZ

1. Seventeen
2. Nine
3. Craig Gordon
4. Virgil van Dijk with 35 appearances
5. Leigh Griffiths with 14
6. Stefan Scepovic with 13
7. None
8. Kris Commons v Inverness CT
9. Stuart Armstrong
10. Celtic 3-0 Dundee United

PAGE 27 - QUIZ

1. They all scored for Celtic via own goals last season
2. Seven times, four SPFL, twice in the Scottish Cup and once in the League Cup
3. Craig Gordon
4. Two
5. None